Prayer for the Sorrowful Brain

Prayer for the Sorrowful Brain

Poems by

Carol Graser

© 2025 Carol Graser. All rights reserved.
This material may not be reproduced in any form, published,
reprinted, recorded, performed, broadcast,
rewritten, or redistributed without
the explicit permission of Carol Graser.
All such actions are strictly prohibited by law.

Cover design by Shay Culligan
Cover image "Rythme, Joie de vivre" (1930) by Robert Delaunay

ISBN: 978-1-63980-755-0

Kelsay Books
502 South 1040 East, A-119
American Fork, Utah 84003
Kelsaybooks.com

for Jeffrey

Acknowledgments

Thank you to the following publications, in which versions of these poems previously appeared:

Apricity: "Alarm at Dawn"
Avatar Review: "The Bird and the Stone," "The Icicle"
Berkeley Poetry Review: "Plastic Factory"
Big City Lit: "On the 6th Floor of the VA Hospital"
Blue River Review: "You Were Born"
Cape Rock: "Lunch with Your Mother Who Is 81," "Mirror Nonet"
Devilfish Review: "The Haiku"
Doubly Mad: "A Goodbye Under Snow-Wet Cover"
El Portal: "At the Precipice of Spring"
Evening Street Review: "Adirondack Postcard"
Ginosko: "Dark Language"
Glint Literary Journal: "The House"
The Hollins Critic: "Prayer for the Sorrowful Brain"
I-70 Review: "Maybe Six Robins"
Lightwood: Life and the Arts: "The Shopper"
Midway Journal: "Man in Protective Custody After Walking on Frozen Mohawk River"
The Midwest Quarterly: "Lunch with Your Mother Who Is 81," "Mirror Nonet"
Minute Magazine: "Dissolving the Distance Between You," "Lunch Break in Congress Park"
Pennsylvania English: "Pope Air Force Base"
Pine Hills Review: "In the Weeks Before DBS"
Poetry Super Highway: "Spooky Zoo Sunday"
Punch Drunk Press: "The Appendix"
Round: "Break Room Conversation"
Sepia: "Here with the Rugged Picnickers"

A Slant of Light, Contemporary Women Writers of the Hudson Valley: "Laid Off Summer"
A Thin Slice of Anxiety: "Root Canal," "That Winter"
Tittynope Zine: "What If"
Trailer Park Quarterly: "Ghost of Ambitions," "The Winter She Left Us for Work in Kansas"
Up the River: "The Ironing Board," "Portrait of a Poet Unhappy with the Size of His Crowd"
Visitant: "Beach on the Great Sacandaga Lake," "In an Office at the Movement Disorder Clinic . . ."
The Wrath-Bearing Tree: "Summer Isolation," "Parkinson's Triolet"

Contents

Prayer for the Sorrowful Brain   15

before

Dark Language   19
Ascend into Blue   21
In Congress Park on a Lunch Break from a Job in Retail   22
Root Canal   23
Public Skate   24
The Haiku   25
You Were Born   27
Plastic Factory   28
Alarm at Dawn   31
The Shopper   32
Laid Off Summer   34
When Workers Decide Union   35
Breakroom Conversation   36
The Ironing Board   37
The Pitch   39
Portrait of a Poet Unhappy with the Size of His Crowd   40
Pope Air Force Base   41
The Icicle   43
Dissolving the Distance Between You   44
A Goodbye Under Snow-Wet Cover   45
Ghost of Ambitions   46
Lunch With Your Mother Who Is 81   48
The Appendix   51
Beach on the Great Sacandaga Lake   53
Spooky Zoo Sunday at Roger Williams Park   54

during

Now Is the Time   59

after

That Winter   63
Mirror Nonet   64
Desserts   65
The Stairway   66
The Walk to Parking Lot C in Late February   67
No One   69
The House   70
On the 6th Floor of the VA Medical Center   71
Parkinson's Triolet   72
The Adirondack Postcard   73
April 10, 2021   75
In the Weeks Before Deep Brain Stimulation Surgery   77
The Porcupine   78
I Gave Birth to a Tree   79
At the Precipice of Spring   80
Man in Protective Custody After Walking on Frozen
    Mohawk River   81
In an Office at the Movement Disorder Clinic While the
    Neurologist Experiments with Different Levels of Voltage
    to Your New Implants, I Try to Assemble an Eight-Piece
    Plastic Puzzle of the Human Brain   82
The Winter She Left Us for Temporary Work in Kansas   83
The Car   84
Summer Isolation   86
Here with the Rugged Picnickers   87

The Bird and the Stone	89
In Which I Try to Make Sense	90
After the Ice Storm	91
Maybe Six Robins	93

always

In the Streets	97

Prayer for the Sorrowful Brain

What world have you made with your tight
dangle of parts? Let these neurons be knit
again with lanolin-soaked wool, yarn
that's been tinged with sumac, goldenrod

onion skin, mint. Let your sparks become
diamonds, your folds become marble, your
nodules jade. Let your every bit glint
into citrine, amethyst, quartz. You are

a sculpture of jewels you conglomerate
brain, a brooch among brooches! Let
this configuration of fiber and gem be
washed in a gush of medicinal oil

Your stitches are pulsing with color
together   together   together

before

Dark Language

There is a land in me of you where we
began our dark language of miracles
We met as trees, part of a surprising ring
whose shadows shaped a grassy circle

of sun. Tree frogs in my branches trilled
to the squat gray females in yours. The fat
moon sat in our limbs whispering stories
of inversion. Our roots curled over each

other in secret and this is where our hearts
met. For decades this was how we grew
Every spring we complimented each other's
sprightly green, the same bursting excitement

You were there each summer day as we eased
into our lush feast of sun, lounged in leafy
abundance. We let it all go together, felt
the same night chill, heard each other's sugar

cracking into color, sparks of hundreds
of small dyings. We stood with each other's
losses and wanted winter, wanted ice to test us
snow to quiet our days. We gave into

the white silence side by side
There is this landscape in me of you
When I open my throat from under that sky
and speak to your morning skin an ancient

breeze presses against us. Years and voices
fall away, bricks of detail and worry
We are breathing again this sylvan air
birthing the next unknown season

Ascend into Blue

Each moment has its demands
tells me I am not a forest

but I am
I am a garrulous bunch of trees

Every jangle of hand
every downpour of speech

knocks me
clean out of heaven

I climb over and over igneous rock
the cooled volcanic spew

Let me drink from a lavender glass
each night an opulent gulp

Let me rest, shelter my bones
tie dreams to a sturdy post

Your name and mine
I zealously whisper

and whisper until
all of the words have gone

In Congress Park on a Lunch Break from a Job in Retail

Hundreds of white clover are flowering
with purpose. Each small head jiggles

in the breeze and I tell them about the patch
of violets I mow around each summer

that is wider every spring. I tell them
because they're listening about the manager

and her imperious clothes, about her assistant
who picks at her loose threads, drapes

them like a veil over his dusty head
They tell me in their chirping voices

to hold that patch of violets close to me
the eloquent purple, those heart shaped leaves

But the owner, I shriek, *he travels to Tibet*
to meditate on his choice of good fortune

Their green voices ripple with tiny urgency
Our thin roots listen when the cold stone speaks

The breeze picks up, ruffling their spiky petals
Let the hair on your skin listen now

Root Canal

Outside the dentist's building
an audacious dance of tree

A pine, black with rain and
splays of long yellow needles

I am going to the chair
and this tree stands posed

muscles flexed and holding
The tree won't come inside

stand behind the dentist
peering in at my teeth

and wink at me. All the trees
have better things to do

I'm sitting in her branches
now, telling you this

Public Skate

You're ice-skating over a four-year-old
his white helmet shading wide

surprised eyes. Yours lock with his
when you fall to one knee, desperate

to stop the slide, to unavoidably collide
and not injure. *Are you okay?*

said a thousand times in one saying
Uh huh. He pops up, skates off

perpendicular to the flow. You move
with the slow crowd, wait

for the hand on your shoulder, some
siren to pull you from the road. Should you

sit down, quit the small speed built
swinging at the curves? You circle back

to your collision, scene of bumper
scraps and shards of car, when the same

kid, speeding against traffic
zings into a tree-sized skater, swerves

into a backward glide. You blink and recant
your guilt. You were one small smash on this

hacked-up ice, a sought-after hazard
knocked into and risen from and left behind

The Haiku

The Haiku realized
several syllables later
that weather patterns had changed
that she was wearing a bikini
over goose pimpled skin

In a cold blast of starting over
she grabbed a run-on sentence
out of a five-page essay
on the Industrial Revolution
wrapped it scarf-wise around her throat

She knitted a thick dress
out of lines unraveled
from random Wikipedia entries
let the loop and bind of wooly facts
keep her free from artistic drafts

She plucked a hat
from the local section
of her daily newspaper
let minor assaults and drug busts
insulate her scalp

She fashioned boots that looked
exactly as if they were durable
from volumes in Wal-Mart's
book aisle, laced them tightly
to the soles of her mud-stained feet

She started eating pizza
in front of the TV
No more baby salad greens
drifting gently onto her plate
She took to sleeping late
and avoiding mountains

She kept in touch with her sister
haiku, listened to their short
bursts on waterfalls and birds
but took no joy
in the conversations

She longed for work
that was fleshed out
something *how to* or *hilarious*
something *unputdownable* or
authoritative and vast in scope

She started watching sunsets while eating
ice cream and weighing her options. A cookbook
occurred to her during one fiery orange display
A cookbook, she considered, *is something*
to drip batter on, leave open

to the heartbreak of unpredictable grease
A cookbook, she thought, setting down
her bowl and licking her spoon
with lazy, rambling directions
recipes with 17 ingredients each

You Were Born

I laid my head in my mother's lap
She was there because you were born
Someone called her   I was hollow

We sat in the break room of nurses who tended
precarious newborns   their strawberry hearts
I laid my head in my mother's lap

She stroked my hair without disappointment
She spoke softly   told me I was a good mother
Someone called her   I was twenty-seven

I remembered when we never spoke
the years of stubborn silence
I laid my head in my mother's lap

Your brave body pulsed
your whole life in a nearby room
you orchestrator

Plastic Factory

Image collision in grocery store aisle
bowled over by camel-hair coat precise
with a soft plaid piece of fine wool wrapped
nice around his neck, he's stacked
8 high, blue—green—gold
cans of cat food, face of baby white
I buy my food under fluorescence

and drive away in circles always back

to factory's constant clatter humming
noise beneath our skin. Gold-haired
mother wads the cotton in behind
the itch, reads the classifieds 5 seconds
at a time to buy a new used car
How many highway miles
did she walk? *Damn thing died!*
It was 5 below zero. To the ceiling
high with cardboard boxes, Jesse smiles
with his 5 kinds of pens and 9
tools for every job. We rest get by
with one pair of cutters and a knife
He tells me, tells me, tells me
15-minute times just so how to trim
the plastic traffic lights

My body shivers like this car's engine rumbles and waits
I see his face inside the round red blinking out, this white
dusk air freezes cars to crunching slow motion

Would she think him a fool? This
curlicue woman in university lounge
Her small car crippled she stamps
her clean leather boot, then couch-slumps
weary, finals time agonized, then phone
grumbles sweetly; dad will pay
for parts. Carpet on the floor
beneath her boots and white
clean white paint on walls, cushions
soft and clutter nice, whir
and chink of copy machine, my circles
blur and every student a QC
inspector, marking down the other's
words—red sticker, red sticker
red sticker my brain

This old black car is humming nice as I drive away back

to Bubba's T-shirt always ripped
One round patch of pick flesh skin
like a window as grease black hands
raise, pull finger thick link, cube of steel
swings slightly upward. My machine
chunks open, releases a part
I cradle warm plastic, break away
gate like umbilical cord, my knife
trims the naval. 28 machines
simultaneously open. I cup
spirit's thin flame like a match
until clock boss clicks, pushes

us free, dark fumed mist
metal mother released
I breathe, like new, this air

I drive away in circles through a clogged tumble of city
up and out through gradations of civilization

and emerge to hilltop's dark
stillness. Evergreens point
in silence. Moon, sweet curve of light
I am home

Alarm at Dawn

When the riotous clucking of chickens
careens you from sleep at 5 a.m.

you find yourself barefoot
in wet grass, struck by the sight

of a bronze fox leaping in gorgeous pursuit
of zigzagging chickens, dizzy with fear

and while you love the fox, her grace and fur
her pulsing hunger, you shout *Hey!* As if

you had the means to harm her
The fox split-second turns, dances like a good

sport into the black woods. The birds
have fled to separate corners and straggle

slowly back, clucking softly for reassurance
One hen has lost what looks like half her feathers

in a damp clump, a monument to survival
It's okay now, you say, tossing feed

but their chicken brains are ruffled
take till noon to smooth back to routine

that business of pecking at the ground
flocking together, the everyday

laying of delicate hope
inside a resilient shape

The Shopper

The Shopper, in her long struggle
to return home, is confronted

by shampoo choices, while the Hair
limp and lusterless, never

opens her mouth. It's for the Shopper
to push past the hunched-over woman

the obstructive cart, decide which
bestows the most beauty for the cost

Her brain begins frothing
She begins rinsing it off

She steps through the sunless rows
tiny canyons of deceptive wind that buffet

from every ingenious direction
She is forgetting, becoming a child

that daydreams of the post-shopping
quarter in her palm, the round crunch

of appeasement sugar
Asparagus, she whispers

leaning deeply into her cart
let's blow this crazy joint

The celery has started weeping
She retraces her steps again

searching for that last
elusive item, its secret aisle

Laid Off Summer

That July the raspberries grew
like slow fireworks, long arcing

branches that tangled into fruit
I scratched my way to the red

globes, ruby princesses, shy
smilers dangling with thorns

It was the over-pruning two years
before that caused the explosion

that wealth. I'd squat in the wet grass
and peer into brambles, spying

out ripeness, reach in for the light
squeeze that, if ready, pops

them off with no stem. Scarlet
shades piled in the bucket. Those

delicate plumps, those seedy drupelets
I struggled not to complain at abundance

the daily, hot chore of collecting
and storing. I'd pour cold raspberry

sauce over the gray folds of my brain
let the sweet tart soak and stain

flavor me bright red and less bitter

When Workers Decide Union

Because 28% more
is the child's calm cheek cupped
in your providing palm

Because house, home, roots
digging into nourishing soil
nourishing air in return

Because when unchecked power
of employer becomes
sublimely, humanly checked

the food full on your family's plate
tastes every day like sunrise
Because 31% more, 55% more

because 26% more, because
worry not vibrating your floors
threatening quake

Because their nuclear greed attempts
mushroom clouds everywhere
Because our sky, our children, our lives

Breakroom Conversation

She tells us she screamed at one
black-eyed mouse. I don't mention
>   *my walls are teeming with rats*
>   *they chew my insulation*

She shivers when she tells it: the mouse
zipped out when she moved her stove
>   *my rats leave droppings*
>   *10 times the size*

We lavish her with comfort and suggestions
she nods at our group politely
>   *my rats scurry with impunity*
>   *underneath my skin*

She listens to talk of traps and basements
agrees to the universality of pests
>   *my sister rats and I are in council, I serve*
>   *them tea and listen to their rodent stories*

When reconciled and done with advice, we walk back
to our cubicles, our quiet clicks and worded tasks
>   *my hair becomes an ancient forest*
>   *buttressing my storied head*

The Ironing Board

hasn't left the closet in years
She sneezes at her own dust
clatters on to the damp mop
about the old basement laundry
the joys of never being collapsed

I used to hold things, she says
She goes on about the iron
and that tricky heat, the ashtray
the cigarettes with their
smooth spirals of smoke

the diet Pepsi always tinkling her ice
The Ironing Board was essential
and sturdy in her time
her crossed T-legs held up
countless indeterminate moments

Every day she stood
in front of that washer and dryer
like exact proof of mother
Now she's given up her dream
of a new wardrobe of linen shirts

She makes a dash for it one spring
cleaning afternoon, lets her sturdy legs
take her on a giddy, hobbling flight
No one hears from her for months
There's an uncomfortable hope

that she's made it to the edge
of town has found some peace
or repurpose at the city dump. She
turns up eventually in the park feeding
chunks of bread to indigent ducks

I miss the cigarettes, she says to a mallard
and the Pepsi and the melting ice. She
leans back against the sun-warmed bench
The iron was kind of a bastard, she breathes
folding and unfolding her legs

The Pitch

What if Emily Dickinson's rise
to poetic stardom was a reality TV show?
Think a Victorian house with staid, heavy
furniture, a white figure wisps across
a distant hallway, cut to a bee hovering
studiously over a patch of red clover

Characters will include Absolute
Silence, Wind (sometimes soft
sometimes wailing), Death, and
a rotating cast of flowers and insects

Emily herself has stipulated
we can only film her in passing

Each confessional is a poem—
ink spreading on paper—
abandoned in various scripted spots
discovered by the camera lying, say
amidst the debris of a finished breakfast

Portrait of a Poet Unhappy with the Size of His Crowd

His ears were new in town but he
had been listening to them all his life

His hair had receded into these ears
disappeared entirely from his head

The mustache that lived on his lip was
a healthy much-loved dear, a deliciously

pampered only child. He could open
his mouth, lift the mustache lid and tell

you everything about his teeth. He came
up my stairs dreading niceties, introduced
himself as a caricature I wanted to erase

At our wedding reception his brother
exposed himself to the bridesmaid

while an earthquake toppled honeymoons
in the tropics. We moved into a moldy

home furnished at bargain prices
Mornings I drank strawberry daiquiris

in a soft blue bathrobe and wrote poems
about nausea. He died first and

I had his mustache removed in one
piece. I wanted to see if it could fly
I wanted the casket closed

Pope Air Force Base

When my father came home
from Vietnam I wanted a doll
one dressed in colorful costume
message from a far-flung culture
I loved those dolls, loved
to touch their storied fabrics
I loved to hold each country's
name on my tongue: *Scotland
Germany   Thailand   the Philippines*

When my father came home from
Vietnam, he brought my mother
a black eye. He brought home
a man who, when he drank
I had to learn to sit still
and quiet as a doll, had to aim
to become not-a-target

He brought home a new room
a secret door
that as I touched it
was not allowed to feel

Sometimes the door opened at night
in the middle of flannel pajamas
sometimes in the scrubbed kitchen
graham crackers on a Saturday plate
The door lurked like a constant raven
peering over my ponytailed head
and when the silent latch lifted
when the door swung wide
war broke out like fiery terror
somewhere in our ranch-style
Air Force base house

Across the street another father
lavished his barbed souvenirs
and another down the street and
one two blocks over, and while
the unquiet dead were never
laid out bloody and real across
our hopscotch military streets
still we felt them, still we became
children of that same unnecessary grief

The Icicle

In the depths of winter
the snow finally became an icicle

Her lifelong dream: to grow by melting
to be clear in her intentions

to stretch thinly from a fat start
wield a formidable spike

to overhang the bareheaded
walking in and out of doors

and silently threaten

In the deep freeze of winter
she perched and hung heavily

gusty winds trembled her length
Complacent in her mass she blinked

slowly, blank with certainty. Everything
would happen: the bright shine

and steady drip, the slow loosening
the sun's hot gaze, her perfect

daring leap, the jarring crash

Dissolving the Distance Between You

for Marly and Josie

Pour water over the deeply frozen earth
skate deftly across the divide

Boil maple sap in the open air
the aroma a soft lure

Aim your arrows at flocks of words spoken
but not meant, follow the path of strewn feathers

Measure the gulf between you with an inaccurate ruler
one that shifts scale between atoms and stars

Nap in the full sun, let the sprouting grass rise
through your bones, wake up side by side

Collect pebbles, the close attention to ground
will bring you to the same stone

Talk to the wind, forget what you're looking for
touch the petals of flowers with no thought
for a vase, give up ever arriving at the door

It's the black crow intoning from a seed of dream
That's the syllable that will save you

A Goodbye Under Snow-Wet Cover

My hat collects a layer
stopping to hug her
I'm under white all day

tucked inside safety
stuck by this storm until
sundown. They won't stay

Goodbye, I say, *have fun, drive safe*
Advice they don't need
to follow the white road

south, then west, sampling
everyone's weather
I want to ride secretly

in their backseat clutter
Goodbye. I open an atlas
trace a line from New York

to Tennessee to Los Angeles
My sky is losing light and
opalescent clouds gather

They call from a bright climate
I'm willing to transplant
their fresh green sprigs of words

my windblown snowscape

Ghost of Ambitions

You come visiting
through the black air
My table pushed against
the window you sit

across, you bob the licorice
tea bag in your bone
china cup. I can't see your
face but hear you

breathe, your gruesome
exhale. The moon has lit
the field but the forest
that surrounds remains

dark. You're crowding me
You've pushed me to
an edge. My womb cringes
You pound this broken

table with an ugly bang
You keep me from sleep
when all I want is blithe
surrender. Do you think

of my unanswered
letters? Do you care
that the mailbox leaning
by my frozen road

is stuffed with disinterest
You don't listen, but rise

and toss me in the snow

Lunch With Your Mother Who Is 81

Her small white turtle head
You look across at her elderly shrink
She asks you how old
your mother-in-law was when she died

You squeeze your spongy brain
74, maybe 76

That's how old my mother was
We were stationed in California

She mumbles something next
as if she's speaking out of mist
Through the murk and tangled vines
You see an outline of her lumbering thoughts
>*four small children, the money, the distance*
>*she missed her mother's funeral*

When my father died, she says
back completely to the table and lunch
Mike was, and here she straddles
worlds again, being here and not
ten eleven, you kids, six years apart

Right. The Jorgensons watched us. You're slipping
too now because you know that's not their name

No, in correcting you she's clear, *not*
the Jorgensons

The Fiorittas, you say, thinking
of the drunk, the father, Benny

Sue Fioritta looked in on you kids

How long were you gone?

A few days, she stares at you. You watch
the lines vertical to her pinched lips
zeroing in on her mouth
and suddenly you're five years old
alone on a sunny street
crossing from your empty house
to the house of the family looking in on you
Captain Fioritto is there alone
sitting heavily in his upholstered chair

Sue made you a pie. You loved pecan pie

She's told you about this pie. You only
remember Benny in his fat chair

She takes a sip from a spoonful
of lobster bisque. *I love pecans*
she says, but *I can't eat pecan pie*
She takes another prim sip, *It's too sweet*

She's made it to the other side of her story
is on firm, remorseless ground
You stand stunned in the middle
of that deserted street
wearing those damn knee socks
feeling the bright burn of the sun's disregard

The Appendix

The Appendix believed she was part
of the large intestine. She didn't have
an origin story. At digestive tract meetings
she dangled silently, sometimes
they forgot to leave her a chair
She had ideas for departmental
improvements but knew she needed
more clout before she could speak
At parties she hung at the edges
of conversations, contributed comments
that no one bothered to hear

She was in love with the liver
but who wasn't, that dark whale
of an organ. *You are beautiful
and vital,* she told herself
They would be lost without you
She wasn't getting any younger
She knew that
She threw herself into the task
of harboring digestive bacteria
She harbored impeccably
She harbored with zeal

until she harbored the wrong crowd
No one answered her calls to 911
That's just typical, she said
in her first bitter tone. She swelled
in self pity and found comfort
in her smarmy new friends
Everyone's got some good in them
she rationalized
making room for a few more
When finally someone noticed
when the bright light of attention

held her in its glare she capitulated
almost violently. *I'll be good*
she sobbed, *I didn't mean it*
she pleaded, but the handcuffs
were already clamped to her wrists
The large intestine pulled back
from the commotion, the bad taste
I knew she'd be dragged off
someday, whispered the colon
as her wails trailed off in the distance
and a thick hush fell over them all

Beach on the Great Sacandaga Lake

> *In 1930, the Conklingville dam closed its valves and filled the Sacandaga Valley with 38 billion cubic feet of water to control flooding on the Hudson River. Over a dozen hamlets now sit at the bottom of the Great Sacandaga Lake.*

Children are building cities
in the sand
All of them have rivers

They pull buckets of water from this lake
that is secretly a river, make rivulets
that satisfy their god complexes

I don't like you! yells a girl
at a boy who has interfered
with her creation

The sky is a tumult of cumulus
and thunderheads
chasing across the blue

A woman pulls a banana out
of her tote, peels it for a toddler
who is drenched and shivering

The wind shouts at the wide
surface of water
and the water answers

Spooky Zoo Sunday at Roger Williams Park

Snow White's crying in front of two zebras
who stand sleek as not caring

Mr. Incredible's buff as a plush bulldog
Superman's three feet tall

GI Joe stands in fatigues soft enough
to sleep in, watches the pumpkin being carved

Witches are handing out yo-yos

The place is crazy with princesses
in cotton candy gowns, and pirates
some well-dressed, some dressed in gore
Nobody's swashbuckling

An angel visits the python, a bride points
at the one penguin outside, a cowboy
likes the fruit bats, SpongeBob is holding hands

A moon bear is chewing
on a pumpkin, a pumpkin is resting
in her mother's arms

A giant frog and tiny lion watch the new giraffe's
long-legged, frolicking dance

Curious George beside the crouching wallabies
is reduced to a small boy from the waist down
His furred legs are resting in a stroller

Someone scalped a clown near the long-necked turtles
stuck the rainbow curls in the back pocket of their pants

Glenda and Dorothy in a little red wagon
are off to see the harbor seals
Minnie Mouse is tired

The golden lion tamarins are huddled in a corner
A blue dragon is by the enclosure where bison hide

It's the flitting fairies with their
pastel wings that break the spell

reveal us as hearts beating behind
bone, our names unadorned

during

Now Is the Time

Let the patriarchs heave and explode in their
last gasp of insecure power; they are dying

Their hearts are beating out of sync
with our future; they are rotting

Their grip among the boulders, their anchorage, is slipping
Now is the time to witness that last vigorous rush of activity

In their gushing love for profit, they are rushing about
filling their near-infinite golden cups and some

soon tomorrow they'll be buried. We'll stand at their graves
and murmur about their just-days-ago revival

The good brown earth will swallow them
The fertile meal from their bones will feed nations

When their houses are cleared, their furniture repurposed
their medals melted back to pure, once we've sorted

and recycled and dumped and burned and donated
and there is nothing left of those fetid foundations

we will regain ground. We need sunflowers eating
their toxin. We need new fields of varied wildflowers

we need the jump of meaty rabbits, the thick hum of bees
the crazy lives of dragonflies darting through our air

We who have been coddled and bathed in honeyed water
we who have been outcast and neglected, who in our shunned

state have reveled in resilience, we tell the ones still fighting
the war is resolved. The patriarch is mortal and dead

This is the rebuilding. We are connected by the same color
of our blood. We are connected by the same air in our lungs

by the bone in our precious skulls. We are connected by our
same mouths born rooting for the same sweet milk

after

That Winter

After the long snowmelt
the ground froze and we walked
over the brown grass like
cement, unforgiving

and the moon rose like
a full radiant pearl
that melted nothing. We sat
all in our separate chairs

and told our disparate
stories. The wind repeated
herself: cold & cold
& cold & cold. We blinked

against frosted cheeks. Some
of us knew the story
that would call a softer
wind. They were still cradling

it's newness. They were still
nursing its hunger. What could
we do but wait, let our breath
warm our frigid fingers

Mirror Nonet

I
let you
go, untie
your bright bound soul
hospital gown strings
I unknot gently in
your sleep, like a child released
you never know until in those
last thin gasps, you rise with relief, be-
gin to swing free. We tell you *peace*
we tell you *embracing sweet*
Then a lean fear snags you
that lifesaving claw
you believe in
we all do
but death
wins

Desserts

As a girl, her mother served her
blackberry pies and chocolate cake
treats from her work at a bakery
Every dinner had a decadent dessert

and after evening meals your mother
would tell you, moistening her thin lips
that she hated her mother's confections
those clouds of sweet filling her child's plate

Her eyes shone with delight at her own
bitter resolution not to bake. Instead
your mother gave you fudgsicles
and sundaes. She kept bags of candy

in a kitchen drawer. You ate your mother's
variety of sugar without question
without history, digesting nothing
but her tacit encouragement to defy

The Stairway

The Stairway to their bedrooms
folded down her steps and slid away
to her own children. The gap
she left they filled at first

with chocolates and red wine
The Stair's lost complaints
began to waft up from floorboards
She'd call late at night and hang up

Caller ID said *Unknown,* but secretly
they knew. They placed a ladder
outside their window, climbed
the wooden rungs to finally sleep

After enough time she sent
a postcard from her family vacation
Enjoying the sun and surf, she wrote
They never vacuumed her enough

They let their kids play too hard
against her slant. Someone set
and neglected a tall Ficus in her
old spot. They expected her

to visit but she was busy
leading to other rooms
rooms they never understood

The Walk to Parking Lot C in Late February

The sun is visible above the horizon
and the sight of it and the blue

is shocking. I saw it from
the fourth-floor window but to be

out from behind glass, it's as if
rescuers had persevered in digging

through the rubble of gloom
and I was buried for enough

days to make my continued breath
an unreasonable hope but the rescuers

had chugged on and supporters prayed
and dreamt of my smudged face

being uncovered from the dark and now
all at once, my weak limbs are cradled

in fireman arms, lifted and
set gently upright into the day

The edge of snow has shrunk with age
the layered history of storms laid bare

The sidewalk weeps, a wobbly line
between melt and dry. I walk slowly

in the parade, wave to the cheering
crowd; the naked trees and shining

ice, the sun blessing my head
confetti of jubilant light

No One

No one's seen you since that long night in the hospital
but it's the holidays and every year we gather
arriving at your door in the barnacled boat
of our good intentions. You greet each of us and

in the moment, can't muster interest. I stand in your
perfunctory hug, notice again that you're shrinking
and I'm solid. I pull a green seedling from your quiet
throat. We stand apart, arms dangling but

Christmas dinner won't eat itself. As the clatter
of dinner stumbles around seasonal decorations of joy
we become nourished with no memory of eating
What's left are stones to scour and arrange

I'll return to that unmarked sculpture like a grave
When we say our goodbyes, you're missing

The House

Her basement is filled with snow
She is standing on her stairs, twisted
around the railing, squinting at packed
whiteness. One window streams light

enough to sparkle. She creaks up
the spiderweb stairs, walks
across the snow beneath her floorboards
She needs to check the attic

Has her roof split along the edges
unfurled its tinny petals? Is she
standing at the mercy of the sky

On the 6th Floor of the VA Medical Center

Finally disarmed, my father curled
in his hospital gown, a large, stiff
fetus facing north. His left hand
would, almost in a rhythm, brush
his face. I pressed the button
on his bed to find his weight
to mark time: 164.3, 162, 159
I rubbed his back, but he rocked
away, he wanted no distractions

What eddy was swirling him
What boat carried him
those last miles? Was he
commanded to lay down
his arms? Did he volunteer
empty solemnly his pockets
and socks, pull the grenades
out of his mouth, drop them
with relief into the deep, black sand

I sat by a window that overlooked a dull stretch of Syracuse
and watched his mammalian exit. I cried. There was no one
in that wide hushed room that could order me to stop

Parkinson's Triolet

I cup the base of your skull, catch
precious cells spilling out like salt
that seasons your limbs, your unholy lurches
I cup the drumbeat of us, miscatch

the rhythm, drop plates with a crash
You feed pills into the widening fault
My palm on the back of your head catches
our precarious marriage, heavy with salt

The Adirondack Postcard

The Postcard *is* the rain
dimpling her mountain lake
She's the two blond oars

embracing lightly on the dock
She's the cluster of red chairs
turned to a private center

damp knees almost touching
She's the thin tap of water
breaking its own tension

The Postcard knows that the boat
is gone, that somewhere
it rests easily against another

dock. She's waiting
the whole picture of it
If she leaves the scene now

only the chickadees would care
shaking drizzle from their black heads
She had intended her arms for the sun

had carved out a wide bowl for cradling
that warmth, but in this picture
it's clouds that inhabit her sky

She sighs and lays down against the bracken
and drench, grows long seaweed hair
She sinks in with the root and rock

the black alchemic soil, and listens
to the boulder's endless stories
those glacial epics, the layers of melt

April 10, 2021

My elusive son and I are meeting
my parents at their hotel. We enter
their double king room and Ted
sits on one unforgiving bed
while Mary sits on the other
hobnailed bedspreads, words
tightly knitted and purled
She puts down her crossword
pen. He holds onto a half-empty
pint of gin. I ask for a drink
and he says, *We'll have to go*

get more. We both think
of the streets below, decades
away, the struggle of navigating
a strange town. Not now
we agree, later. Now, my son
and I leave to explore. I trail
behind him to the elevator
The hotel is crowded. We squeeze
into the narrow space, shoulder
to shoulder. Before the door
closes, I see tables with unfrozen

frozen bagels, coffee urns, bowls
of tiny plastic non-dairy creamers
Free food! I say to my son. He says
Let's wait for something better
The elevator takes us to the highest
floor, and it is dazzling: ceiling
and walls of glass, glints of light
freckling the scene. A crowd is gently
milling, there's a buzzing, animated
hum. Snow-covered mountains
rise to the west and a crisp

fresh air. I spot long tables
of breakfast: fresh bagels, less
bitter coffee, small pitchers
of cream. Again, I say, *Let's eat*
and while I lay hungry in my
crumpled blankets, the cold
morning reddening my nose
my son says, *No, not yet*
This answer keeps me
with him, with these travelers
for one more breath

In the Weeks Before Deep Brain Stimulation Surgery

Dried leaves skittering like toads across the lawn
after last night's wailing storm that downed trees
and electric cables leaving us to skitter down
the streets with these trunks cut just to the white

line of the shoulder. Your shoulder next to mine
you rise to rows of prescription canisters
these pills that stand in for diminishing cells
In two weeks, they will test you stripped of that

scaffolding. You say sometimes you delay your
medication to get a taste of total withdrawal
to feel the teetering start of collapse. The heavy frost
is melting and I pack candles and flashlights back

into our power outage box, the box I assure you
is well stocked, the one I promise not to lose

The Porcupine

Squatting in the hungry tree the Porcupine
sits as if she is just these sparse gray branches
just the November night between. Even held
in a sharp flashlight beam her camouflage

is complete until she shuffles, flips her short
tail. Her plump shape dawns in your
observer's brain and she becomes
a windfall, a secret, an ungainly reason

to hope perched in a spindly tree. She wants
you to stand beneath her, open your
promising arms, to call for her to jump
and while you both recall her newborn quills

she tumbles softly into that cradle as if good
fortune rested against you as happy to be held
by you as you are to finally embrace that
animal belly, the warm unfamiliar heft

I Gave Birth to a Tree

I gave birth to a tree, which no one
mentions, and this opened
up in me a great silence

Decades later, leaves are growing
roots are growing. There's no
end to being a mother

When suddenly my hand
holding the pen startles
fingers freckled with

innocence, *a wild*
furred creature
a stillness opens

That's how we meet
among those branches

At the Precipice of Spring

On either side of this frozen mud path
are sculptured monuments to winter

Each storm's snow
     that fell distinct
  was melded by
surface thaw and drip
  that wended its way
    as water to the ground
chanting through the
      layers, the bright trickle
    slowly compressing
      time and

now this frigid air has snapped the softness
back into rigid place, soot-studded and drawn

Today is routine. We cause harm to each
other and exist harmed. To survive, I

commute. I begin here in the dim light
in the hum of the dominant conversation

of trees, my brain balanced precariously
my fingernails cracking

Man in Protective Custody After Walking on Frozen Mohawk River

I walk on the ice of my pleasures
I walk between miracles and confusion
I walk inside a rose
                     —Adonis

I'm making my way over
ice not a cool slick foot
thick hardened slab that keeps
drowning inaccessible but
these jammed broken
chunks floating in the air
of metal gray running water
the soles of my feet stabbed
by this frosty jagged ground
they're shouting at me the
trees they lean against stand
bare branched and silent
I hate that I'm here that
exhaustion will compel me
to something more reason
able the river's dark depths
call to me and if my inflamed
rage could be heat that fires
my skin and melts this ice I
would sink through and swim
with this ribbony body along
pebbles until ocean until
the sound of salt until I am
washed and lifted wave
by wave onto sparkling sand

In an Office at the Movement Disorder Clinic While the Neurologist Experiments with Different Levels of Voltage to Your New Implants, I Try to Assemble an Eight-Piece Plastic Puzzle of the Human Brain

The stubby screws
in the cerebellum
poke out, exposed
to the cold
air. I have to leave
these parts to nestle
in the temporal
lobes, untethered
It's the best I can do
which means I can't
put the brain
back on its base
I have to leave
the puzzle upside
down on the counter
brain stem tilted
toward the doctor
who asks you again
to open and close
your left hand

The Winter She Left Us for Temporary Work in Kansas

While we hunkered down under early storms and frigid air, while
we crunched through days of squeak and bladed wind, while
our windows filled with white, and streets became trenches
that locked cars in treacherous battle, as we braved our way
to work and store, she endured
the caress of a warmer wind and pined for northeast cold

While we emerged from one collective heave of ice only
to be plunged into the next harrowing dump of snow, while
we trailed with docility behind lumbering rust yellow plows
praising the salt they tossed, the trembling feeble paths they made
she brushed her hair in sunlight
and dreamt of catching snowflakes on her tongue

While we peered out of caked, bleak eyes, our boldness
eroded, our skin weary of bracing, our lank arms stuffed
into padded sleeves of defeat, she flew home to our dusted-over
dirty white and rejoiced at the forecast of the next day's storm
"I love to shovel!" she exclaimed
"I missed the snow!" she swooned. We silently killed her

The Car

The car of herself has been disassembled
wheels lain sideways, one in each corner

against the front lawn. Gleaming bumpers
set down, pressed into the mowed grass

There's the body of her planted in the middle
plunked immobile to the spot. She is otherwise

completely in parts and not to gawk
but the countless metal bits are arranged

with maniacal precision as if a strong
magnet at her center would compel

each one to click back to its old spot
Her mechanic is young and aloof

but she trusts his skill. They have to sell
and the question is—whole or in parts?

She suggests bolt by bolt is too much work
He looks away. *You'll have phone calls*

she says, *people coming over. Sell it in one easy chunk*
But she never considers the meticulous reassembly

It's up to you, she says, *but what I would do
my vote, is to sell it whole.* His response

is not to look up and she notices again his
windy silence. She's sure now he'll sell by the part

What she'll have in the end is a lighter
model stripped to essentials
motor   gas   a sense of direction

Summer Isolation

I paint the porch with strokes of blue
diamond. By sunset, it's a veranda

of green and you have fallen asleep
at the shore of a lake that glaciers through

your dreams. You wake with stones in your
teeth and ice melting under your skin

You arrive home with feet delighted
by the verdancy at our entrance. We

dig holes in the ground, nests for roots
the width of thread. You shake ancient

drops of water off your bones. When
a ruby-throated hummingbird zips past

we see it

Here with the Rugged Picnickers

and the woman in her yellow T-shirt with her blue-bladed
oars and red canoe, her daughter at the prow, her son
a few feet away in his neon-green, child-sized kayak

They stay close to shore, skimming through
the choppy water. She doesn't wear
a life jacket but the children do

Rain threatens, wind whips, the sky is stingy with its blue
In the car the news was all virus and rising numbers
The news was all death tolls and shortages

The wind pulls my hair out behind me. I sit beside a small creek
that ripples through muddy green until it hits the sand and rocks
near the lake, rocks the size of field mice, of turtles, of cows

resting on the ground. The woman brings her canoe to shore
and her children wander between the rocks in bare feet
They jump back and forth across the creek. The girl

wades into the lake up to the bottom of her
skirt. They keep their life jackets on, and a mother
duck drifts by with at least a dozen half-grown chicks

At this picnic table I've gathered my deceased parents who
took me to picnics by the lake with a canoe and my
deceased son, our newborn who never left the hospital

An inchworm with thin black stripes along its green length
is doggedly exploring the picnic table's potential, pulling
itself up to its full height, swaying back and forth, searching

for an upward hold that doesn't exist. My parents are silent and
seem happier than I remember. My son, who is the most expansive
tells me the trees are used to picnics with the dead

that an inchworm is an inchworm, regardless

The Bird and the Stone

The bird followed the stone into the ground
She loved him. She thrilled him with songs of flight
Her small head rested on his round back. Her
wing brushed his heart. Together they would heave

and sink. Together, listen to the soft lives
of toads and worms. He was her cottage, she
was his nest. They lived in a generosity
of roots. They plunked memories down in neat

cemetery rows, epitaph after epitaph
The winter the stone died, the bird shook
the dirt from her wings and laid him
at the bottom of an icy creek. She

hopped on the snowy bank
and watched him shine

In Which I Try to Make Sense

for Bernadette Mayer

If the lancepor is laciporous
let me whine that note
as crashing loud and wide
as any hurricane ever

If yelling the amhilt of my
doothwan pulls a single vein
from the body of miscreteness
I have songs for the laciporous stage

to let out the pus
of the lancepor, to
punt bubbles from
one season to the next

The late September sun
is heating the corner of my
netspar, my bloma is swizing
up in torsion. Where is the rock

and bone of plonce while the worst holds
the gemdig on overfed shoulders, while we
aim at knocking it off, while that sea of bodies
stretches on for generations and pulses and breathes

After the Ice Storm

When the tree falls on your car and you've
known the tree for 22 years, it's trunk and height

it's cedar bright smell, it's branches that once
held your bantam rooster crowing at 4 AM

while you flung shoes at its cocky dim shape
that kept the snow off the bottom corner

of the driveway and hid the house enough
from the busy road. The car too you've known

for 80,000 miles, the car that made
the long commute almost bearable

that came to you after your father died
your father who had two accidents

in two years in the new car he bought after
your mother died, the second accident

happening during a mini stroke that didn't
kill him but led to a mysterious decline

that led you to ask the doctors to stop
trying, and the money your father left

made you think to buy a new used car and
here was this Prius at the dealer priced

unusually low for a two-year-old car
with 9,000 miles but it had been in two

accidents with its previous owner who
you imagine, was in their 80s like your

father, crashing their last car, so the car is
family and the tree and they've both gone

together. Maybe you'll plant a lilac
bush in its place at the driveway's end

and there will be a new car and it will always
be the car you got after the one you

got because your father died, the one that
was smushed end to end by the trunk

of the old, cherished tree and you'll say

Remember the tall tree, the fuel-efficient car
the father whose love was a pine needle drink

Maybe Six Robins

       are swooping
             onto and
taking off
       from the wobbly thin
            branches just outside
      the window over my kitchen sink

This is about berries and early fall

       but they don't say this
           to me   They don't say

           Carol, you loaf about with your pen
and your pajamas
      while we   *harbingers of spring*
    are performing circus acts
        while eating

            they just keep launching
   and alighting
         the branches swinging wildly
with every landing
         and departure

I sit in my heavy skin
and sip an elixir

      to hollow my bones

always

In the Streets

We are still in the streets
        a glut of protest
We are still stopping the subways
        blocking all traffic
We are still in the streets, we've never
        stopped marching
        our arms still uplifted
        our signs piercing
        the sky with words we will live by
We are still in the streets
        our anger is exponentially expanding
        a deep ocean current pressing us forward
        our vigilance is unceasing, a many
        eyed creature, we are asleep
        and we are watching
We are still in the streets
        our guttural roar a tidal wave
        rushing, a foaming wall
        growing, erupted from the clap of fear
We are moving across landscapes
        a determined respect gathering
        of countless shapes and shades
        and constructs of love
We are still in the streets
We are a sonic boom of voices
        our words have flown past the atmosphere
        collided with the pulsing stars that have changed us
        we have changed the shapes of the stars
        we mirror the mutinous constellations of peace
We are still in the streets
We are an acceleration of evolution of culture
We are rattling the rusted bars of cages

We are shaking loose the profit from jails
    shaking loose the profit from war
    shaking loose the profit from the 1%
    We are sewing those dollars into inviolate
    blankets we place over the shoulders
    of anyone who is cold
We are still in the streets
We are pounding the windows
We are shaking the ground
We are vibrating the air
We are pouring out and washing over
We are that force of love and water
We are submerging what is not laced
    with compassion
We are still in the streets
We are still shouting
You can hear us in the pulse of your blood
    pumping forward
We are still in the streets of our homes
    and our jobs and our fields and
    our alleys and our schools and our
    woods and our skyscrapers
    and our mountains
We are plotting and stomping and marching for peace
We are still in the streets

About the Author

Carol Graser is the author of the poetry collection *The Wild Twist of Their Stems* (FootHills Publishing, 2007). Her work has been published in many journals, including *Apricity Magazine, The Berkeley Poetry Review, Evening Street Review, Hollins Critic, I-70 Review, The MacGuffin, Midwifery Today, So to Speak, Southern Poetry Review,* and *Midwest Quarterly.*

In 2003, she initiated a monthly poetry reading series at Saratoga Spring's legendary Caffe Lena, which continues to gather poets and poetry enthusiasts some 20 years later. Graser's dedication to this series has fostered a strong community of poets and has helped to make Caffe Lena a central hub for poetry in the area. Graser often reads her work at rallies, fundraisers, and poetry events in the area and has run poetry workshops for teens and at-risk youth. She lives with her husband in the Adirondacks of upstate New York where they raised three children, countless chickens, and a few cats.

www.ingramcontent.com/pod-product-compliance
Lightning Source LLC
Chambersburg PA
CBHW022015160426
43197CB00007B/451